Caring for Animals

Written by Marilyn Woolley
Series Consultant: Linda Hoyt

WorldWise
Content-based Learning

Contents

Chapter 3

Conservation 12

Chapter 4

Helping animals in the wild 18

Chapter 1

Animal caretakers

All over the world, people have jobs caring for animals. They may work in zoos, **sanctuaries**, national parks or **aquariums** and feed, water, brush, bathe and exercise animals. They also clean and fix their cages. They check to see if the animals are sick or hurt and they play with the animals. Some caretakers may study the animals they work with to learn more about them.

Find out more

Here are some more places where people care for animals:

- animal hospitals
- veterinary clinics
- kennels
- animal shelters
- stables
- grooming shops
- **wildlife refuges**

Can you think of any more?

Think about ...

What would you do if you found an injured animal? When you finish reading this book, check to see if you would do something different.

5

Caring for aquarium animals

Aquariums are zoos for animals that live in water, where they are kept in large glass tanks filled with water. Aquariums help people to look after the ocean by teaching them about the animals that live there.

Working at an aquarium

This is an interview with David Donnelly, who works at an aquarium.

Q. What do you do at the aquarium?

A. I am a diver who looks after the sharks, eels and other animals in the big tanks. I prepare food for the animals and put it in the tanks in the best place for them to find it. I go underwater to feed each of the sharks and stingrays. I also check the water temperature and that the water in the tanks is clean. Dirty water can harm the animals, so I have to clean the tanks. Sometimes I also give talks to groups of children who visit.

Q. Do you do work outside the aquarium?

A. Yes, I am often asked to help out with research in the open ocean. I have also flown over the ocean to find and count blue whales off the southern Australian coastline. I help tag ocean animals. The tags have **radio transmitters** so that scientists can track where the tagged animals travel.

Q. Do people at the aquarium help sick animals?

A. Yes. I helped an injured sea turtle recover at the aquarium recently. I fed it and gave it medicine. Once it was strong enough to be released I tagged it and put it back into the sea. I have also helped in the rescue of other sea animals. When whales become stranded on the beach, I go with a team of people to try to get them back into the water.

Chapter 2

Behind the scenes at the zoo

A zoo is a place where animals are kept so that people can learn more about animals, their behaviour, and their **habitats**. Zookeepers care for animals in zoos; the list below left shows the kinds of things zookeepers do every day. Zookeepers also answer questions visitors have about the animals and they sometimes help scientists study the animals they care for.

Daily duties of a zookeeper

- food preparation
- feeding
- watering
- grooming
- bathing
- exercising
- cleaning **enclosures**
- repairing enclosures
- observing animals to see if they are sick, upset or hurt

Naomi Sharp the zookeeper talks about taking care of the animals:

You need to love animals to be a zookeeper. It's a lot of hard work. Most of my job involves cleaning the animals' enclosures, making them healthy food and making sure the animals get enough exercise. Some of the animals need a lot more care than others. I usually look after elephants. With their big meals and big stables, can you imagine how much mess elephants make?

My biggest challenge is making sure the animals don't get bored, so we set up training sessions and programs to keep them busy. I'll do things with the elephants like blowing water, kicking balls, riding them and running with them to keep them exercised. Sometimes elephants can even help out around the zoo. The elephants and I have been asked to help move heavy logs for new enclosures. These activities are all about making sure the animals are fit, healthy and happy.

The best part of my job is getting to know each animal and being able to share its life.

Feeding time at City Zoo

You can see some of our animals being fed or playing with the zookeepers at the times below. Check out the chart to see your favourite animal!

	Baboons	Giraffes	Elephants	Red pandas	Lorikeets	Pelicans
Monday	11:00am	11:30am	12:00pm		12:30pm	1:00pm
Tuesday		11:30am		12:30pm		
Wednesday		11:30am	12:00pm		12:30pm	1:00pm
Thursday	11:00am	11:30am		12:30pm		
Friday		11:30am	12:00pm		12:30pm	
Saturday		11:30am	12:00pm	12:30pm		1:00pm
Sunday	11:00am	11:30am	12:00pm		12:30pm	

	Servals	Macaws	Tortoises	Orangutans	Tigers	Penguins
Monday						
Tuesday	11:00am	12:30pm				2:30pm
Wednesday				1:30pm		
Thursday		12:30pm	1:30pm		2:00pm	2:30pm
Friday	11:00am					
Saturday		12:30pm		1:30pm	2:00pm	
Sunday		12:30pm	1:30pm	1:30pm	2:00pm	2:30pm

Map of City Zoo

Entrance/Exit

Otters	Gift shop	Sea lions
Orangutans	Penguins / Pelicans	Baboons
Meerkats		Tortoises
Giraffes	City Zoo Cafe	Red pandas
	Lorikeets / Macaws	Servals
Lions	Elephants	Tigers

Otters	Lions
1:30pm	2:00pm
	2:00pm
1:30pm	2:00pm
	2:00pm

Meerkats	Sea lions
	3:00pm
2:30pm	
	3:00pm
2:30pm	

Chapter 3

Conservation

Why have zoos?

Zoos play an important part in animal **conservation**. The chart on the next page shows the many ways that zoos help to preserve animal species.

Zoos have often been criticised for keeping animals in unnatural environments. However, people who work in modern zoos have improved the way animals are kept, creating **enclosures** that are like an animal's natural **habitat**. They also make sure that each animal has the right food and that they don't get bored.

Find out more

By becoming a friend of your local zoo, you can help the zoo care for animals. Many zoos are part of **global networks** that work to protect **endangered** animals.

Find out what the people who belong to these groups do.

Old zoo enclosure

New zoo enclosure

By raising money to help with conservation projects in natural environments.

By taking care of sick or injured animals so they can go back to the wild.

By studying animal behaviour so the needs of animals are better understood.

How zoos help conservation

By reintroducing animals into the wild where they are endangered or **extinct.**

By educating people so they can change their behaviour to help animals.

By setting up breeding programs for animals that are endangered.

By educating people about animals and their habitats.

Saving Asian elephants

The Asian elephant is an endangered animal. It was once common throughout India and Southeast Asia, but today fewer than 50,000 live in their natural habitat of grasslands and forest. They eat leaves, grasses and shrubs. They need a large area of habitat because of their great size and the amount of food they eat. Every day, an adult elephant eats up to 170 kilograms of food. Much of their habitat has been cleared for logging, farming and houses and this means less food and less space for the elephants. Poaching is also a major threat to elephants – many are killed for their ivory tusks.

Because they are trying to save the Asian elephant. some zoos have set up breeding programs to help the Asian elephants mate. Zoo workers include trails in the enclosures to try to match the elephants' natural habitat. By trying to meet their needs, zookeepers hope elephants will have many young.

Think about ...

What do you think about keeping animals in zoos?

Watching elephants at zoos

Some zoos have webcams that show what elephants do all day at the zoo. Online visitors can see what the elephants do behind the scenes, when they are not on public display. Visit the Smithsonian's National Zoo and the San Diego Zoo websites.

Saving wolves

All types of wolves are endangered animals. The number of wolves in the wild has dwindled as the places where they live have been taken over by people and cleared for logging, mining and roads. Many wolves have also been hunted and killed because people are afraid of them and do not understand them. Other wolves have died because of diseases.

But people know that wolves are facing extinction, and many zoos have started conservation projects to help them survive.

Case study: Red wolves

The red wolf became extinct in the wild in 1980. But there were red wolves still in zoos, so scientists began a breeding program.

By 1987 four pairs of red wolves were vaccinated against common diseases and reintroduced into the wild. The scientists placed a **radio transmitter** on each wolf to study its movements. The red wolves began to breed in the wild within a year. This was a good sign, because if an animal breeds it means that it is healthy and comfortable in its environment.

Many groups of scientists were involved in breeding and releasing red wolves. The hard work of animal caretakers in these conservation projects has meant that the red wolf now has a chance to survive as a species.

Find out more
The red wolf was once common throughout the southeastern United States. Find out how red wolves live in the wild.

Think about ...
Think about all the things people do that take over the habitat of animals.

Chapter 4

Helping animals in the wild

Raptors

Raptors, birds like owls and eagles, are birds of prey. Most raptor species need a lot of space to find food and nesting sites, so many raptors are threatened when their **habitat** is destroyed. Sometimes raptors are injured by vehicles. Bruised or broken wings leave the birds unable to fly, hunt or stay safe. Sometimes raptors are harmed when they are hunted or poisoned. People have formed organisations around the world to work towards the **conservation** and survival of raptors.

The next page shows how people care for raptors at raptor conservation centres.

Raptor conservation centre

Did you know?

Some birds have to stay at conservation centres for the rest of their lives because their injuries have left them disabled. They would not survive on their own if released into the wild.

1. When a bird is admitted, veterinarians examine it. The bird's injury or illness is treated.
2. A bird may have several weeks of intensive care in a small cage. It stays in this cage until its injuries are healed.

3. When the bird's health is improving, caretakers move the bird to a medium-sized cage. Then it can stretch its wings with short flights.
4. Once the bird is nearly recovered, caretakers move it to a large flight cage where it can fly further.
5. If the bird is strong, healthy and taking care of itself, it is released near the place it was found.

Orangutans

Orangutans live in the tropical rainforests of Borneo and Sumatra in Southeast Asia. They are under threat because the rainforest that is their habitat is being cut down for farms and mining. Some young orangutans are taken from their mothers and sold as pets. This is illegal because orangutans are a protected species, and many orangutans die when treated this way.

People who have formed organisations to help save orangutans work in national parks in places like Indonesia.

Local residents and people from around the world work for these organisations. They hope to educate people everywhere about the plight of the orangutan.

Workers study orangutans to work out how to best help them. They **rehabilitate** orangutans that are sick or too young to care for themselves. Rescued animals from around Indonesia are cared for until they are strong enough to be released into the wild.

Orangutans are rehabilitated in the following way:

1. They are taken away from the people who have them illegally.
2. They are quarantined to make sure they have no diseases.
3. Babies go to the nursery to be cared for. Young orangutans go to a halfway house where they can act much as they would in the wild. Older orangutans go to an **enclosure** where they learn how to behave like wild orangutans.
4. When the orangutans can care for themselves, they go to island **sanctuaries** where they can roam free.
5. Orangutans that cope on the island sanctuaries are released into the wild.

Helping an injured animal

What do you do if you find an injured wild animal? First, make sure the animal really needs help. Look at the checklist below.

Fact

People often don't know how to care for wild animals properly. Always got advice from an expert.

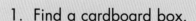

Signs that an animal needs help
- It is brought to you by your dog or cat
- It is bleeding
- It has a broken limb
- It is a bird with no feathers, or only a few feathers
- It shivers
- Its parent is dead

Now you are sure. What do you do?

Now, call an expert at a **wildlife refuge**, a **humane society** or a zoo. They may tell you to keep away because wild animals can be dangerous. But if the experts say it's okay, ask an adult to follow the instructions below to help the animal.

1. Find a cardboard box.
2. Punch holes into it from the inside out.
3. Put soft cloth like an old shirt into the box.
4. Put on gloves.
5. Cover the animal with a towel.
6. Scoop it up gently and put it in the box.
7. Do not give it food or water. Food or water can harm a sick animal.
8. Put the box in a warm, dark, quiet place until the animal rescue workers arrive or until you can take the animal to a wildlife refuge.

Glossary

aquarium ponds or tanks where living animals and plants are kept and displayed in water

conservation to act to keep things like animals, plants, landforms or buildings in their natural state

enclosure an area that has fences or other barriers to keep animals in a space

endangered in danger of dying out

extinct a species of plant or animal no longer living on Earth

global network communication among individuals and groups around the world

habitat a place where a plant or animal naturally lives

humane society an organisation that helps sick or abandoned animals

radio transmitter a device that uses radio signals to send information about the location of animals

rehabilitate to care for an animal until it is able to return to the wild

sanctuary a place where plants and animals are protected and cared for

wildlife refuge a place that offers animals protection from harm or danger

Index